illuminature

WIDE EYED EDITIONS

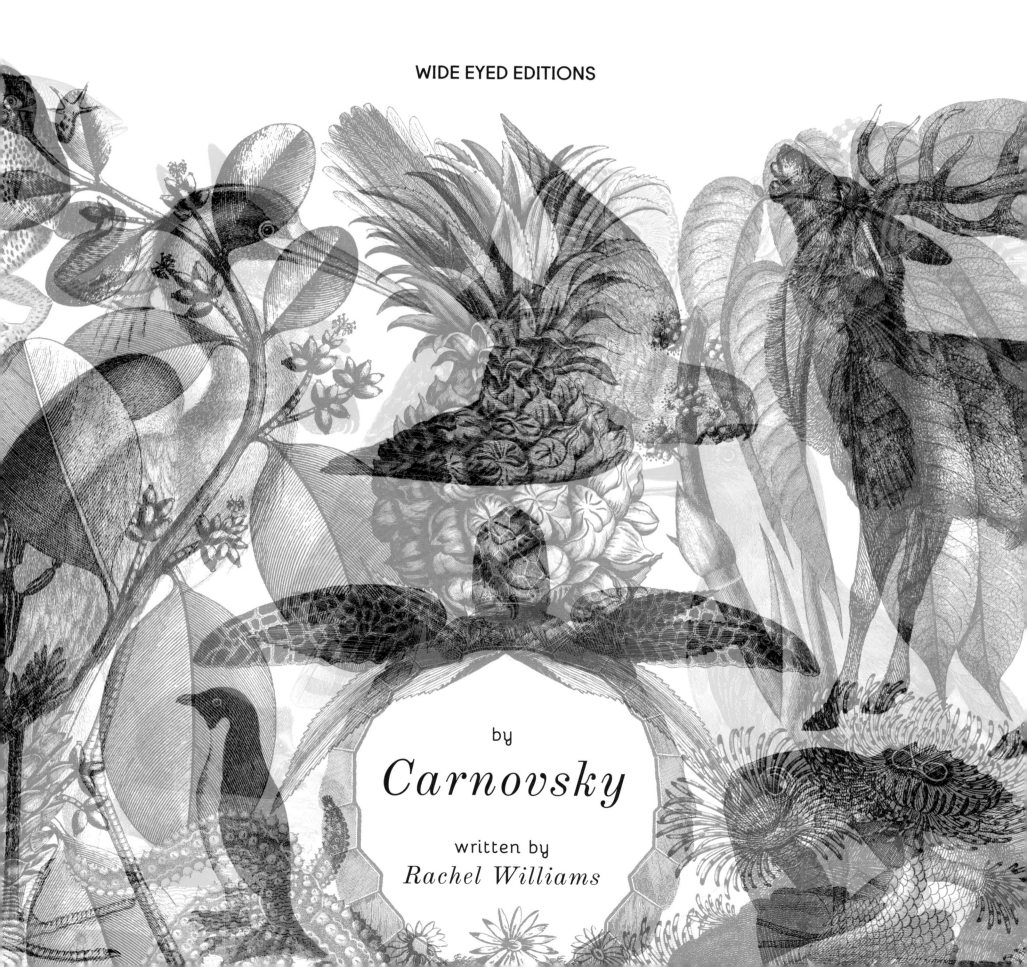

by

Carnovsky

written by
Rachel Williams

nature
never
stops

With every tick of the clock, an animal wakes up and goes out in search of food.
The sky might be dark when the creature first stirs: nighttime is ruled by the
nocturnal animals. During the light of day, *diurnal* animals
like to hunt. And as the world welcomes dawn, or bids farewell to the day at
dusk, *crepuscular* creatures appear. These animals may have evolved
to see in the dark, or to sniff out a meal in the dim light of dawn and dusk,
or have defenses that prevent them from becoming someone else's meal.
Whatever their unique ability, each creature chooses to emerge at a certain
hour each day for one key reason: *survival*. Nature is illuminated
by the amazing survival tactics of animals.

Who will you find on your
journey through the wild?

CONTENTS

*Travel through the pages of this book to uncover
extraordinary animal behavior in ten destinations.*

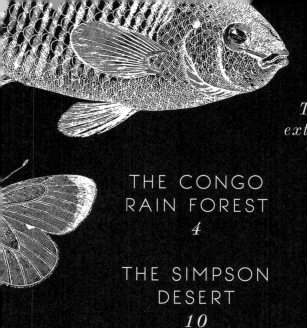

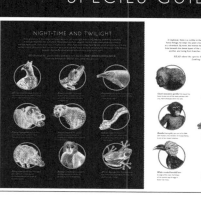

HOW TO USE THIS BOOK

DESTINATION

Travel to each *destination*
and discover key facts about
every habitat.

THE OBSERVATION DECK

See which animals you
can spot from
the observation deck.

SPECIES GUIDE

Then turn the page to learn
more about each species in
the *species guide*.

Take the **red** lens to see
which creatures roam
during the daytime.

Use the **green** lens to
light up the plant life of
each habitat.

Looking through the **blue** lens, discover
nocturnal and crepuscular creatures which
are harder to spot in the dark.

THE CONGO RAIN FOREST

The tropical rain forest covering the Congo Basin in central Africa is teeming with life. At more than 750,000 square miles, it is the world's second-biggest tropical rain forest, and is home to some of our planet's most skilled hunters. In places, only one percent of sunlight is able to reach the forest floor, making a meal hard to find! From the tiny *Charaxes* butterfly, which seeks out nectar with the many smelling receptors on its body, to the African leopard, which stalks the forest prey on soft-padded paws, every creature that lives here has evolved to have special adaptations that help it navigate the jungle's shadows.

WELCOME TO THE RAIN FOREST

Destination
The Congo Rain Forest

Continent
Africa

Countries
Cameroon, Equatorial Guinea, Gabon, Democratic Republic of the Congo, Republic of the Congo, Central African Republic

Habitats
Forest, Freshwaters, Grasslands

Size
772,204 square miles

Who lives here
400 species of mammals, 1,000 species of birds, and 700 species of fish.

NIGHTTIME AND TWILIGHT

Many predators in the Congo rain forest are more active at night than during the day, preferring to hunt by moonlight than face the sun's heat. These creatures have adaptations that make them perfectly suited to navigating the dark: some have special night vision, others have razor-sharp hearing and smell, while others still rely on their sense of touch to feel out the dark spots of this dense forest. As dusk descends, the first to stir is the African leopard – but which other animals follow him to hunt in the dark?

READ about the species below and then turn back to THE OBSERVATION DECK. Looking through the BLUE lens, what can you see?

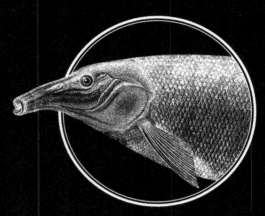

African crowned eagle This bird of prey swoops through the forest at speeds of up to 99 miles per hour.

Dwarf crocodile The smallest member of the crocodile family in the world, this reptile sleeps in burrows during the day.

Elephant fish This fish uses the electric organs in its tail and nose to locate its prey in dark, murky waters.

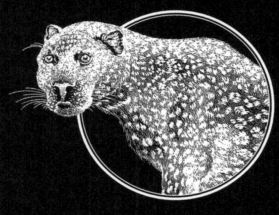

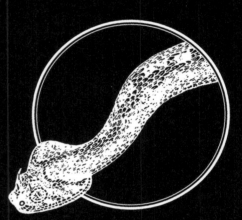

Pygmy hippopotamus To prevent its skin from cracking, this miniature hippopotamus wallows in mud.

African leopard This spotted cat of the Congo is most active between dusk and dawn when it hunts in the shadows.

Gaboon viper The fearsome viper's excellent camouflage allows it to hide in leaves while waiting to spot its prey.

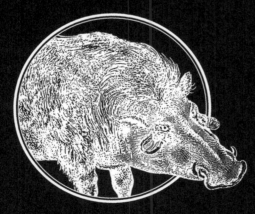

Hairy giant forest hog The biggest of the different wild pig species, this hoofed mammal can weigh up to 600 pounds!

Hamlyn's monkey Also called the owl-faced monkey, it is known to travel by foot on the forest floor.

African big-eyed tree frog With huge eyes and a camouflaged body, this frog is a stealthy shadow hunter.

DAYTIME

At daybreak, there is a rumble in the jungle as a giant mountain gorilla awakes. Thundering through the thick forest foliage, he steps into plain view. At nearly six feet tall, he is the biggest male in his group, and is known as a silverback. By noon, the intense heat is too much for his troop, and they, like many other animals of the forest, hide beneath the dense layers of the canopy to cool down, while the youngest of the troop climb trees, chase one another, and swing from branches. But the gorillas aren't the only animals to look out for during the day.

READ about the species below and then turn back to THE OBSERVATION DECK.
Looking through the RED lens, what can you see?

Giant mountain gorilla This king of the forest is also one of the most precious, with only 700 individuals left in the wild.

West African forest gecko In 2010, four new sub-species of this spiky, stripy reptile were discovered by scientists.

Charaxes butterfly This brilliant orange insect spends much of its time in the highest canopy of the forest.

Bonobo Sharing 98.5 percent of its DNA with humans, this member of the ape family is one of our closest relatives.

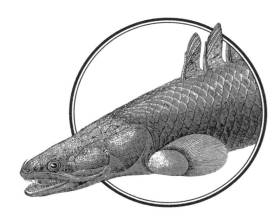

Birchir This ancient fish has a row of protective scales on its back to fend off the bite of numerous ferocious predators.

Western gorilla The most common great ape of the forest, the western gorilla is known to hunt with tools such as rocks.

White crested hornbill With its large white crest, the female of this species lays its eggs in forest tree holes.

African forest elephant This forest-dwelling creature is the smallest species of elephant, and travels in groups of up to eight.

Mandrill These Old World monkeys travel in troops and communicate through scent markings, vocalizations, and body gestures.

THE SIMPSON DESERT

An endless sea of red sand and blue sky, the Simpson Desert stretches across the Queensland, Northern Territory, and South Australian borders, making it the world's largest sand dune desert. This is a true wilderness, where life seems impossible, but even here animals survive in surprisingly diverse and unusual ways. From the brilliant, white wildflowers to the tiniest Eyrean grasswren, the cycle of night and day is strictly observed by all living things, as they collect water from condensation at dawn and hide from predators in long spinifex grasses during the day.

Destination

The Simpson Desert

Continent

Australia

Country

Australia

Habitats

Desert, grasslands

Size

68,000 square miles

Who lives here

200 bird species, at least 34 native mammals, 13 kinds of fish, 125 reptile species, and 22 species of amphibians.

NIGHTTIME AND TWILIGHT

Most of the desert's logical dwellers begin their day when their greatest threat has gone to bed: the sun. Of the creatures that burrow underground or take shelter in the desert's long grasses during the day, the desert bilby is perhaps the most particular land engineer. This miniature marsupial keeps hot air at bay by plugging the hole to its burrow's entrance. Another, the Australian grass owl, sits openmouthed, releasing heat from its mouth cavity to keep it cool while it perches in one of the desert's only tree species, the gidgee, on the lookout for its next meal.

READ about the species below and then turn back to THE OBSERVATION DECK.
Looking through the BLUE lens, what can you see?

Desert bilby With powerful arms and an acute sense of smell, this long-tailed marsupial digs for meals of insects.

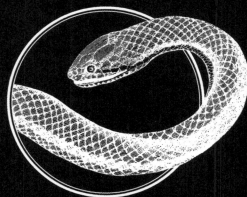

Inland taipan Preying on rodents, this fierce snake inhabits the cracks in the dry earth of the desert's soil plains.

White-striped mastiff This tiny bat lets out a high-pitched sound when hunting to direct others toward a meal.

Short-beaked echidna This spiny anteater has a pointy snout that can sense electrical signals from prey.

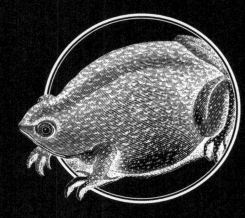

Water-holding frog Named for its ability to store water, this frog can move water from its bladder to its mouth!

Australian grass owl This nomadic owl has been spotted in the trees of the Simpson, hunting in the desert's darkness.

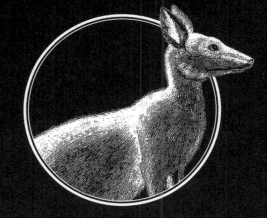

Red kangaroo This herbivore has an Achilles tendon that acts like a spring, recycling energy with each bounce.

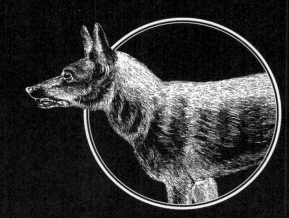

Dingo The legendary wild dog of the outback hunts alone and in packs, traveling great distances to find food.

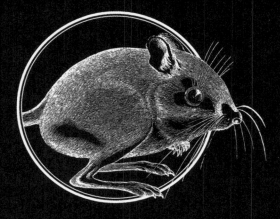

Spinifex hopping mouse Hiding in desert grasses, this rodent can raise its body temperature to make its habitat feel cooler.

DAYTIME

As the sun's rays appear over the sand dunes, the desert's daytime hunters wake up. Lizards, like the perentie and the bearded dragon, are active throughout the hottest parts of the day, moving rapidly over hot surfaces of sand and stopping to rest in cooler spots of shade. With strong legs, their bodies absorb less surface heat while running. Other hunters, like the Australian kestrel, have an adapted sense of eyesight that allows them to see near ultraviolet light and detect invisible urine trails around rodent burrows.

READ about the species below and then turn back to THE OBSERVATION DECK.
Looking through the RED lens, what can you see?

Feral camel Feeding on the desert's grasses and shrubs, this camel gets most of the water it needs from the food it eats.

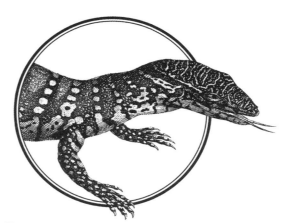

Perentie With a forked tongue that can pick up food scents in the air, this monitor lizard hunts at the hottest and most humid time of day.

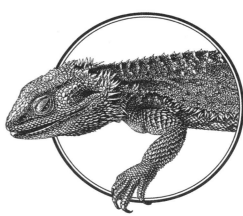

Bearded dragon This desert reptile has spiked scales that change color when breeding or fending off possible predators.

Australian kestrel Having spotted its prey, this kestrel catches its food on foot, dropping to the ground silently before pouncing.

Eyrean grasswren This tiny bird is known to "skip" backward in the sand, to uncover buried food.

Kowari Like some other Australian mammals, mothers of this rat species carry their babies in a pouch. It takes in water through its food.

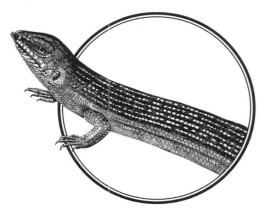

Sand-sliding skink This sprinter chases down its prey. Its light body means that it doesn't sink into the Simpson's sand.

Thorny devil The spikes all over this lizard help to channel water into its mouth when dew forms on its body overnight.

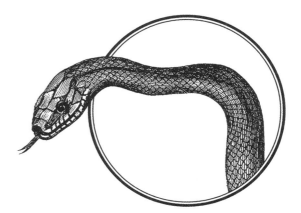

Yellow-faced whip snake This colorful snake is known to have excellent reflexes, chasing and capturing lizards on the run.

LOCH LOMOND

The largest stretch of freshwater in Scotland is also one of the coldest: at night, the temperatures here can drop to below zero in the winter months. The animals in and around the loch are as wild as the myths and legends that surround it: herds of red deer roam freely alongside red squirrels, rutting stags, beavers, hen harriers, and Scotland's prized woodland bird, the elusive capercaillie. More than a quarter of Britain's plant species are found in and around this wooded loch. As night falls, the wood warbler welcomes the dark with a loud call that even the deepest sleepers can't ignore . . .

WELCOME TO THE LOCH

Destination
Loch Lomond

Continent
Europe

Country
Scotland

Habitat
Loch (the Scottish word for "lake"), Woodlands

Size
270 square miles

Who lives here
As one of the most diverse habitats in the United Kingdom, the wildlife of the loch and surrounding woodland number more than 500 species.

NIGHTTIME AND TWILIGHT

In winter, darkness falls early over the loch, but the calm, still waters are brought to life by more than 200 species of night hunters. At nightfall, one of the loch's most charismatic residents, the European otter, stirs and comes out to feed, having spent most of its day in its lochside burrow. You're unlikely to see the otter move over the land to reach the water, however, as much of its travel takes place underground. All night, this whiskery hunter searches for its prey on both on land and in water, as it seeks out birds, frogs, and even small beavers.

READ about the species below and then turn back to THE OBSERVATION DECK.
Looking through the BLUE lens, what can you see?

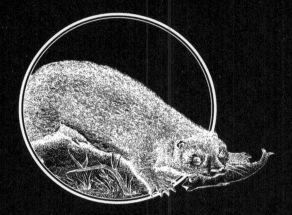

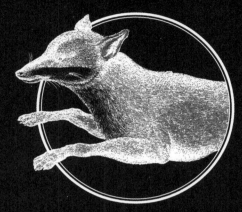

European otter An excellent swimmer, this creature uses its sensitive whiskers to detect prey underwater.

Red fox Cloaked in its red coat, this stealthy hunter has an acute sense of hearing, that it uses to find prey.

Badger This stripy, short-legged omnivore is a forager – it takes whatever meal it can find in the dark!

Hedgehog At dusk, this creature – with its 5,000 spines – can be seen on the shores of the loch, searching for worms.

Wood warbler Named for the song it performs, this creature builds nests in the grounds of the loch's woodlands.

Pine marten Found in trees around the loch, this predator also finds shelter in tree burrows during winter.

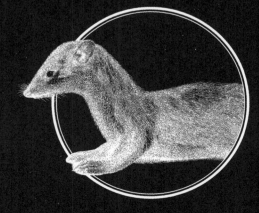

Sea trout This loch-dweller can rapidly change color, getting darker when chased by predators of the night.

Mink This semiaquatic animal builds burrows around the shores of the loch, hunting when the sun goes down.

Scottish wildcat With its exceptional sight and hearing, this rare forest feline hunts by the loch and in the trees.

DAYTIME

As dawn turns to daylight, the prized bird of Scotland, the capercaillie, is beginning its mating display. Positioning himself on a large tree overlooking the loch, the male of the species fans his tail feathers, straightens his neck, and points his beak skyward, waking the loch and its surrounding woodland with a loud, distinctive song. The typical song given in this display is a series of double clicks like a dropping ping-pong ball, which gradually accelerates into a popping sound like a cork coming out of a bottle. Another day has begun!

READ about the species below and then turn back to THE OBSERVATION DECK.
Looking through the RED lens, what can you see?

Capercailllie The largest and loudest member of the grouse family feeds on the protein-rich pine needles of the loch's woodland.

Gray squirrel Introduced from the USA, this creature warns others of danger through a variety of sounds and chattering of teeth.

Red deer Britain's largest land mammal has antlers up to 26 inches long. It has a vegetarian diet, feeding on grasses and leaves.

Black grouse This creature brings a touch of early morning magic to the lochside with its cooing calls and ornate dancing.

Pink-footed goose Grazing on grasses by the loch during daylight hours, this migratory goose spends its winters at the loch.

Golden eagle Powerful, majestic, rare, and elusive, this eagle is a great scavenger and feeds on rabbits and grouse by the lake.

Roe deer The shy deer of the loch's woodland can be heard making short, cough-like barks when alarmed.

Eider duck The eider's nest is built close to the loch's edge and is lined with eiderdown – feathers plucked from the female's breast.

Water vole Most active in daylight, voles dig their own sleeping chambers and underwater entrances to their burrows.

THE ANDES MOUNTAINS

The massive peaks of the world's longest mountain range are a breathtaking sight to hikers and climbers who traverse its peaks, but they are also home to animals of all shapes and sizes. Stretching north to south along South America's west coast, these mountains have permanent residents that have learned to survive its dry conditions, high altitudes, and cold winters. With shorter legs, tails, and ears than many other mammals (this reduces heat loss), and larger lungs that can cope with the lower levels of oxygen at higher altitudes, the majority of Andean wildlife know how to find a meal – at 19,685 feet!

Destination

The Andes

Continent

South America

Countries

Venezuela, Colombia, Ecuador, Chile, Peru, Bolivia, Argentina

Habitat

Mountain, Cloud forest

Size

1.3 million square miles

Who lives here

600 species of mammals, 1,700 species of birds, 600 species of reptiles, 400 species of fish, and more than 200 species of amphibians.

NIGHTTIME AND TWILIGHT

Nighttime in the Andes is the moment when the world's most adaptable big cat comes out to play. The stealthy feline that goes by several names, including mountain lion, puma, and cougar, has one great skill: patience. Because it is not an excellent sprinter or long-distance runner, the cougar relies on stealth and surprise when hunting prey, and traverses the Andes' open scrubland and bluffs where huemul deer rest. Deep into the night, the moment arrives to pounce, and then drag the prey to a secluded area where it can feed undisturbed.

READ about the species below and then turn back to THE OBSERVATION DECK.
Looking through the BLUE lens, what can you see?

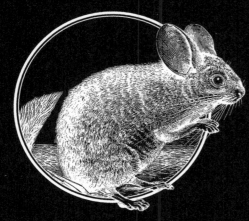

Chinchilla This rodent has poor eyesight but navigates using its whiskers, which are twice the length of its body.

Andean mountain cat Hunting at dawn and dusk, this small feline uses its acute sense of hearing to hunt.

Cougar The mountain's most patient hunter can leap 16 feet, from a sitting position, and jump up to 40 feet.

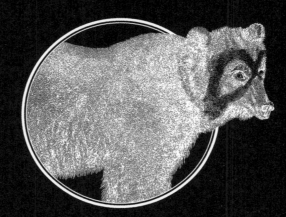

Burrowing owl Active day and night, this owl collects mammal dung that attracts beetles, which it then captures and eats.

Spectacled bear This tree climber hunts at all hours throughout the cloud forest, but only at night.

Andean tapir This tapir has a flexible snout to find food and a thick coat to withstand freezing conditions.

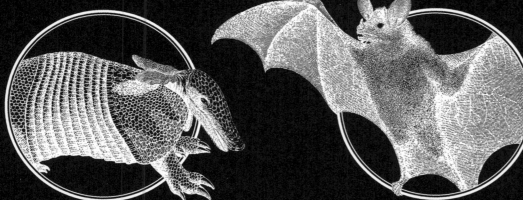

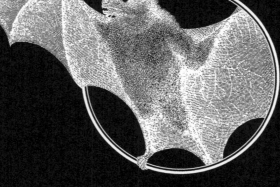

Armadillo The only mammal with a hard shell, this species has a sticky tongue that can reach into termite mounds and anthills.

Peruvian long-nosed bat This bat emits a call that bounces off nearby objects and produces an echo to locate its next meal.

Titicaca water frog This aquatic frog has many folds of capillary-rich skin that enable it to breathe underwater.

DAYTIME

As the sun rises up to reach the peaks of the mountains, the Andean condor shakes its feathers out in preparation for the morning flight. With the world's largest wingspan, this vulture finds the windiest part of the mountain and sets out on it – scavenging for food that has been caught by other animals and left unfinished. Though reliant on other predators for a meal, the condor plays an important role in mountain life, cleaning up after others. Its excellent eyesight means that leftovers are easily spotted in the mountain's broad daylight.

READ about the species below and then turn back to THE OBSERVATION DECK.
Looking through the RED lens, what can you see?

Alpaca Kept warm by its shaggy coat, this domesticated member of the camel family grazes on vegetation at high altitudes.

Vicuña The national animal of Peru alerts family to predators with a high-pitched wail, and attracts mates with a humming, or "orgling" sound.

Andean condor With a featherless head that allows it to feed on leftovers, this scavenger has good chances of finding a meal.

Llama Trained to carry wares for humans at high altitudes, this species is known to hiss and spit when its packs are overloaded!

Coati This stripy-tailed mammal finds fruit in trees high in the forests of the Andes, and on the forest floor, with its flexible snout.

Huemul The endangered south Andean deer is well-adapted to broken, difficult terrain with a stocky build and short legs.

Andean goose This heavily built bird is resident in lakes and marshes of the high Andes, and protective of its territory.

Andean cock-of-the-rock As its name suggests, this bright-headed bird is a show-off, performing impressive courtship displays.

Culpeo The Andean fox is an opportunistic hunter, living off leftovers from other hunts as well as rabbits and other rodents.

WEDDELL AND ROSS SEAS

The polar icescapes of the Antarctic Ocean may appear to be frozen wastelands, but recent studies have shown that the region's ocean is more abundant with life than once thought. Two of its most important zipcodes are the Weddell and Ross Seas. Homes to whale and seal families, these waters are considered to be the world's last example of a healthy marine ecosystem, and a living laboratory for scientists trying to understand the inner workings of nature. With 24 hours of sunlight at the peak of summer and the long dark night of frozen winter, some species still find ways to regulate their body clocks and protect themselves from the cold.

WELCOME TO THE POLAR SEAS

Destination
Weddell and Ross Seas

Continent
Antarctica

Habitat
Seas

Size
Ross Sea: 1.3 square miles
Weddell Sea: 1.08 square miles

Who lives here
Seals, whales, penguins, petrels, albatross, krill, and hundreds of species of planktonic life.

29

NIGHTTIME AND TWILIGHT

From September to March each year, the Antarctic experiences long hours of daylight, peaking in December when there is more than two weeks of 24-hour sun. Mammals such as seals dive in shallower waters during these summer months, when their prey of squid and small fish come closer to the water's surface to feed. But scientists have discovered that seals still feed at "night", following a daytime and nighttime pattern even in 24-hour sun. For some nocturnal and crepuscular animals of this region, however, there are still ways to find darkness. It all depends how deep you dive . . .

READK about the species below and then turn back to THE OBSERVATION DECK.
Looking through the BLUE lens, what can you see?

Weddell seal This seal dives deep and swims back toward the surface so that its prey is backlit by the ice above.

Leopard seal The most formidable hunter of the seal family, this animal feeds on prey that includes other seals.

Crabeater seal Gathering with others around airholes in the ice, this curious seal absorbs oxygen after hunting or playtime.

Black-bellied storm petrel During the breeding season, this monogamous bird breeds nocturnally in colonies.

Snow petrel Antarctica's snowy bird feeds out at sea but breeds on pack ice, farther south than any other bird.

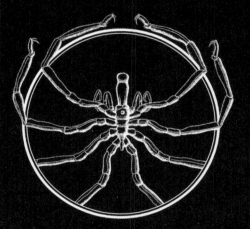

Sea spider Little is known about this species that inhabits dark corners of the seabed, feeding on anemones.

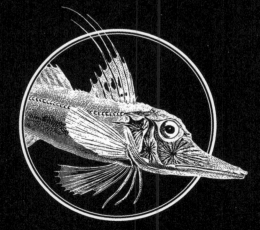

Crocodile icefish The blood of this extraordinary fish never freezes because its body produces a kind of antifreeze.

Southern fulmar This migratory bird nests in a colony on a cliff, laying a single egg on a ledge or crevice.

Antarctic fur seal This seal dives down to depths of 100–130 feet to catch its prey, using its acute sight and hearing.

DAYTIME

Spending a winter's day in Antarctica is like taking an outing to the coldest, windiest, and most desolate place on Earth. Yet at the peak of winter, daytime animals, like emperor penguins, breed. The males endure the worst conditions, looking after the egg on land for months, while the females go out to sea in search of food. There they build up their reserves before returning weeks later with food for their hungry families. Back on land, the males keep warm by huddling in groups of up to a thousand, taking turns to stand at the edges where it is coldest.

READ about the species below and then turn back to THE OBSERVATION DECK.
Looking through the RED lens, what can you see?

Emperor penguin One of the best swimmers in the region, this penguin hunts by gliding through the water at great speed.

King penguin A young penguin cannot hunt until his waterproof feathers have grown, and so he feeds on digested fish from his parents.

Minke whale This curious creature has up to 70 grooves in its throat, allowing it to scoop up prey in big gulps of water.

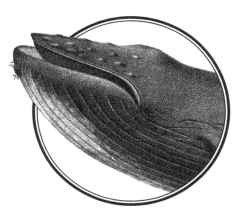

Humpback whale Scientists believe that this whale's songs are used to communicate with others and to attract potential mates.

Killer whale This world-renowned killer of the sea hunts in deadly pods, made up of family members of around 40 animals.

Adélie penguin In autumn, the Adélie walks 31 miles from its onshore nest to reach open water, and returns in spring.

South polar skua This polar bird breeds on Antarctic coasts, laying two eggs in November and December.

Hourglass dolphin The female of this dolphin species nurses its young, which can swim with their mother from birth.

South Georgia pipit The only songbird of the Antarctic builds its nest from dried grass and feeds on small insects and spiders.

THE REDWOOD FOREST

Walking through the ancient redwood forest is a bit like discovering a new city – made from trees. The skyscraping tree species that makes this forest a world-renowned attraction is the California redwood, characterized by cinnamon-colored bark and extreme heights. Animals that live here are varied: some, such as the marbled murrelet, rest in the canopies, while others, like salamanders, stay out of sight on the forest floor. Clever creatures, such as the Sonoma chipmunk, find refuge within the three-foot-thick trunks of these trees, out of sight of passersby . . .

WELCOME TO THE FOREST

Destination
The Redwood Forest

Continent
North America

Country
United States of America

Habitat
Temperate forest

Size
176 square miles

Who lives here
4,600 native plant and animal species, including bald eagles, elk, bears, owls, bats, foxes, and woodrats.

NIGHTTIME AND TWILIGHT

When the sun drops below the horizon, the forest soon turns velvet black. Flanked by the giant trees of the wood, the northern spotted owl welcomes night by breaking the silence: "Woot, woo!", it calls. These owls don't appreciate habitat disturbance, and are known to rest in the same redwood or sequoia tree for most of their adult lives. From this vantage point the owl spots its favorite meal – the flying squirrel. Owls are known to sit completely still and then pounce on squirrels who are mid flight, who are themselves on the hunt for breakfast.

READ about the species below and then turn back to THE OBSERVATION DECK.
Looking through the BLUE lens, what can you see?

Northern spotted owl With a unique mode of flying, this hunter glides silently through the air to snatch its prey.

Coyote This resourceful creature is capable of running at speeds of up to 40 miles per hour.

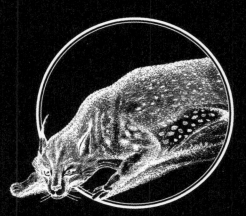

Bobcat The most common wildcat in North America lives alone, hunting prey with stealth and marking territory by scent.

Gray fox A master climber of the forest, this fox can climb tailfirst down trees to catch prey of rabbits, mice, and insects.

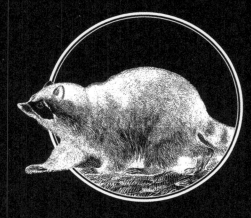

Raccoon This agile stripy-tailed creature uses its front paws and long fingers to find and feast on prey at night.

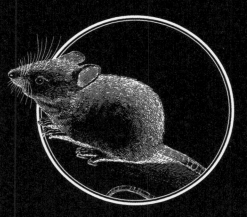

Dusky-footed woodrat Traveling along tree branches, this rodent uses its tail to ward off predators.

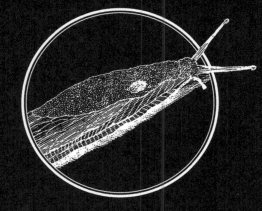

Banana slug Mostly nocturnal, the head tentacles of this mollusk are equipped with supersensory organs to find prey in the dark.

Black-tailed deer Most active at twilight, this species communicates via glands located on its lower legs.

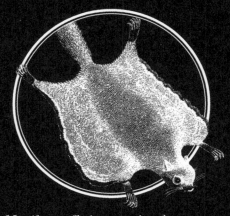

Northern flying squirrel Gliding from tree to tree, this squirrel hunts with large pupils that allow it to see in the dark.

DAYTIME

Daylight in the forest begins slowly, setting light to the giants from canopy to floor. One of the fiercest creatures of the forest is first to stir – the black bear! These powerful creatures have adopted a daytime routine in this forest, and make a symphony of growling and snorting sounds as they set out on the morning hunt. The black bear is an agile athlete: with its short claws and powerful legs, it can catch a meal on the ground or above the forest floor. What do you think it's caught on this morning's hunt?

*READ about the species below and then turn back to THE OBSERVATION DECK.
Looking through the RED lens, what can you see?*

Sonoma chipmunk Mostly active in daylight, the Sonoma chipmunk gathers food in its cheeks and carries it back to its burrow to store.

Marbled murrelet Unlike other birds that nest in colonies, this creature takes to the canopy, laying eggs on moss and lichen.

Bald eagle A fierce predator of the forest, this eagle's eye is almost as large as a human's, but four times as sharp!

Roosevelt elk When predators are in sight, this deer curls back its upper lip, grinds its teeth, and hisses softly to communicate with its family.

American black bear A mother teaches her young to hunt fish and mammals, as well as scavenge for roots, berries, grasses, and insects.

Stellar's jay One of only a few birds in the world to build an intricate nest with mud, this blue bird feeds on nuts, seeds, and acorns.

Great blue heron Wading through streams and rivers of the forest, this bird is an expert fisher, snaring food with a nosedive.

Foothill yellow-legged frog Also found in waterways of the forest, this amphibian lays its eggs in masses attached to underwater plants.

Monarch butterfly The world's most famous migrating butterfly uses its eyes to locate flowers and antennae to sniff out nectar.

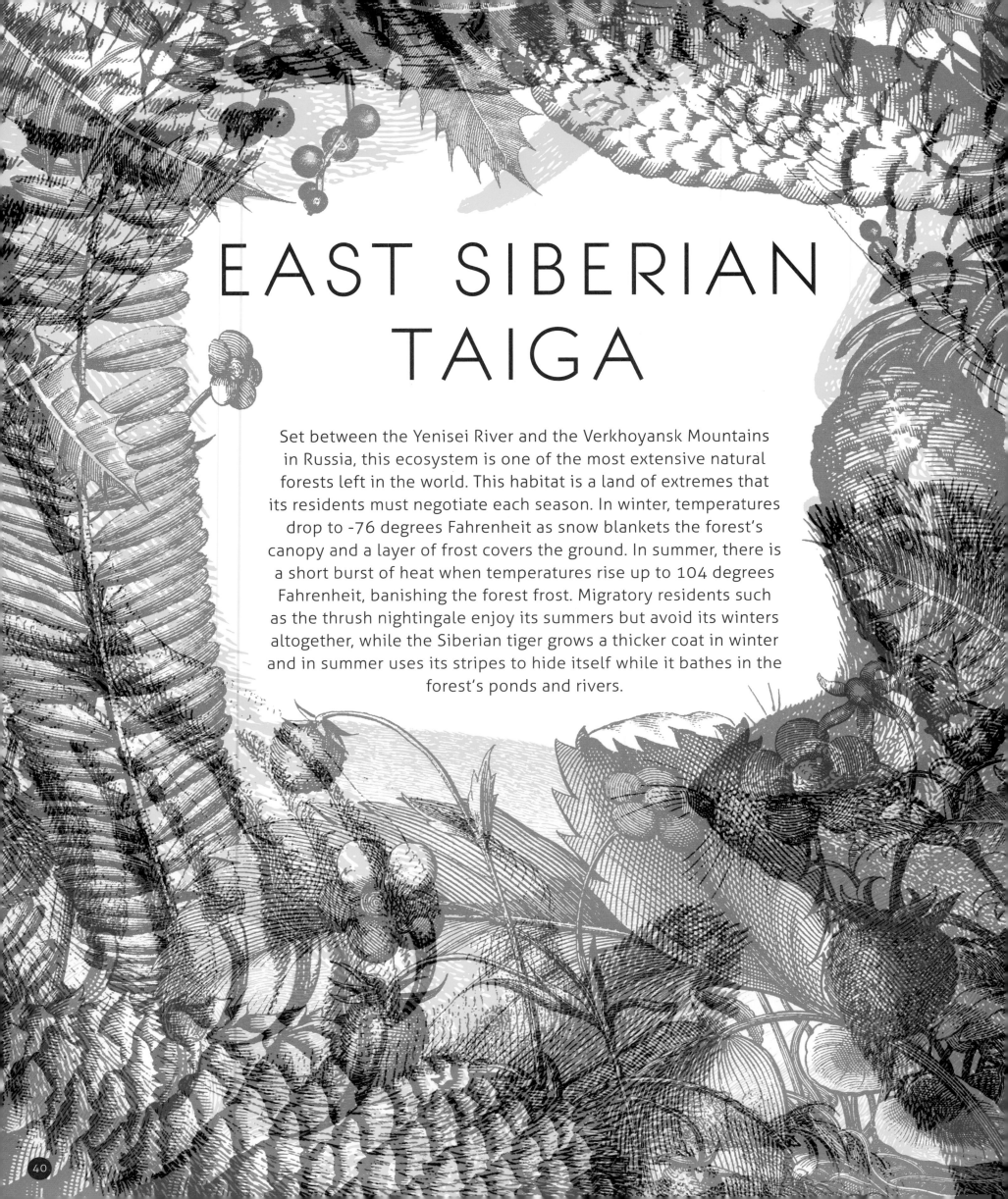

EAST SIBERIAN TAIGA

Set between the Yenisei River and the Verkhoyansk Mountains in Russia, this ecosystem is one of the most extensive natural forests left in the world. This habitat is a land of extremes that its residents must negotiate each season. In winter, temperatures drop to -76 degrees Fahrenheit as snow blankets the forest's canopy and a layer of frost covers the ground. In summer, there is a short burst of heat when temperatures rise up to 104 degrees Fahrenheit, banishing the forest frost. Migratory residents such as the thrush nightingale enjoy its summers but avoid its winters altogether, while the Siberian tiger grows a thicker coat in winter and in summer uses its stripes to hide itself while it bathes in the forest's ponds and rivers.

WELCOME TO THE TAIGA

Destination
East Siberian Taiga

Continent
Asia

Country
Russia

Habitat
Boreal forest

Size
1.5 million square miles

Who lives here
Russia's largest populations of brown bear, moose, and wolf, as well as key bird predators such as the peregrine falcon.

NIGHTTIME AND TWILIGHT

Dusk comes early to the taiga for most of the year, where some of the world's toughest creatures survive. The thrush nightingale, who inhabits the forest for the summer months, begins the night with a loud call, waking the many predators of the forest who take advantage of the summer temperatures to catch prey that have lingered too long before bedtime. In winter, some creatures hibernate, and others migrate, while those that stay, like the tiger, lynx, and wolf, rely on their night vision and thick layers of fur to ensure them a full night's hunt.

READ about the species below and then turn back to THE OBSERVATION DECK.
Looking through the BLUE lens, what can you see?

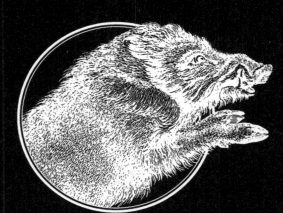

Brown bear Hiding beneath the dark cloak of the long night, this bear ambushes its prey from behind pine trees.

Eurasian wolf When the moon is high, this wolf will howl to its pack, signaling time for the night's first hunt.

Wild boar Hiding in the densest parts of the forest, these boar stir at dawn and use their super sense of smell to hunt.

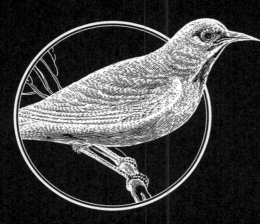

Thrush nightingale The male of this species makes loud whistles, trills, and clicks at night to woo potential mates.

Siberian musk deer With tusklike canine teeth, and long pointed hooves, this deer feeds on lichen at night.

Eurasian lynx This carnivore has a thick coat that camouflages it, changing color between seasons.

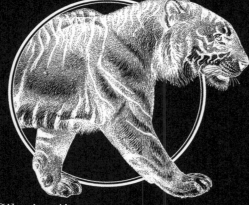

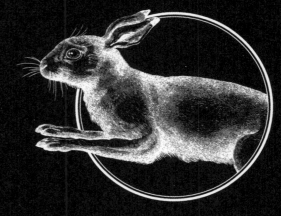

Siberian tiger The thick forest makes this habitat one of the only places on Earth where this tiger can roam and hunt freely.

Great gray owl Perched on a tree, this owl can locate prey moving beneath two feet of snow!

Snowshoe hare White as snow in winter and brown during summer, this hare is the forest's master of disguise.

DAYTIME

The herbivores of this forest also have special adaptations to ensure that food is plentiful, whatever time of the day. Elk are one of the few species in the world that can eat and digest pine needles and spruce needles, which are one food source that is plentiful at all times of the year. Their legs are very long, which helps with navigation in deep forest foliage, and their eyes, positioned clearly on the sides of their head, are their greatest hunting tool. Other daytime creatures, like the peregrine falcon, are also reliant on their razor-sharp eyesight for survival.

READ about the species below and then turn back to THE OBSERVATION DECK.
Looking through the RED lens, what can you see?

Reindeer Roaming wild in these forests, this species has sharp-edged hooves that help it walk on ice or dig for food.

Peregrine falcon With its ultrasharp eyesight, this bird of prey drops down on prey from high up in the forest canopy.

Black stork Stalking the rivers and ponds of the forest with its bright eyes, this red-beaked creature feeds on forest insects.

Hooded crane Nesting in the taiga's remote wetlands, the first hooded crane nest was not discovered by scientists until 1974!

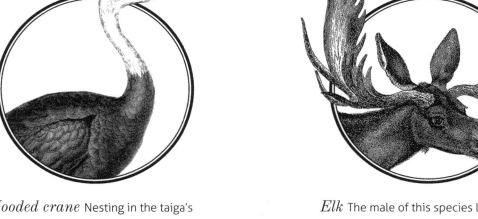

Elk The male of this species loses its antlers in spring, but begins to grow them back in May, ahead of the breeding season.

Short-tailed weasel This opportunistic hunter feeds on the forest's smallest prey: shrews, rabbits, insects, and small fish.

Wood grouse Also known as the western capercaillie, this grouse feeds on the forest's rich vegetation.

Sable With its acute hearing and strong sense of smell, this member of the marten family is one of the forest's best foragers.

Eurasian red squirrel Like its American cousin, this squirrel spends up to 80 percent of its day foraging for food.

THE SERENGETI PLAINS

Named by the indigenous Masai people as the place of "endless plains", the Serengeti is a world-renowned ecoregion. Home to some of the world's best-loved mammals, including the lion and giraffe, it is also a superhighway of animal migration, with wildebeests traversing the grasslands each year in search of fresh greens. During the dry season, water is scarce, and the grasses on these plains have either dried out or been eaten. This lack of food triggers the migration of around two million wildebeests from the plains to the Acacia-Commiphora woodlands. At the beginning of the wet season, these creatures complete the cycle and return to the now-plentiful plains.

WELCOME TO THE GRASSLANDS

Destination
The Serengeti Plains

Continent
Africa

Country
Tanzania

Habitat
Grasslands

Size
11,583 square miles

Who lives here
Around 70 large mammal and 500 bird species, including wildebeests, gazelles, zebras, buffalo, and Africa's favorite cat, the lion.

NIGHTTIME AND TWILIGHT

As the sun sets on the Serengeti, the queen of the cats, the African lioness, stirs from her perch in a tree. Her cubs are nearby, but she is the first to spot breakfast: a wayward blue wildebeest that has wandered away from his herd. There is no other place in Africa that supports such a concentrated abundance of hoofed meat amid such an open landscape, and the wildebeest's poor vision at dusk means that its chances of survival are reduced. The wildebeest is not the only creature on the lion's menu, which are opportunists that will also hunt animals as small as mice up to the towering giraffe.

READ about the species below and then turn back to THE OBSERVATION DECK.
Looking through the BLUE lens, what can you see?

African wildcat This cat uses the camouflage given by its stripy coat to ambush rodents.

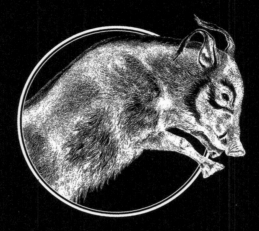

Bushpig This hairy pig is omnivorous (meaning it eats plants and animals), sniffing out meals with its nose.

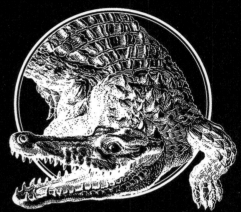

Nile crocodile The largest species of crocodile in Africa, it feeds on zebras and wildebeests from the Serengeti's swamps.

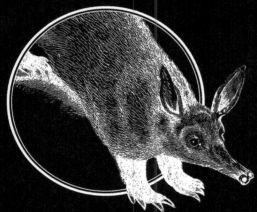

Aardvark Sniffing out a meal of termites in a nearby mound, this long-nosed animal is the Serengeti's best excavator.

African pygmy hedgehog These hedgehogs consume up to 30 percent of their body weight in food each night.

Lion Most active at dawn and dusk, these hunters of the Serengeti can spot prey more than 1,000 yards away.

Greater bush baby This curly-tailed primate has bat-like ears that allow it to track insects and catch them midflight.

Golden jackal The golden-haired canine of the plains is known to choose a mate for life.

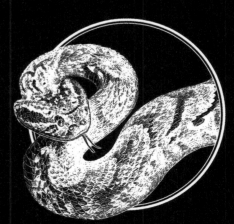

Puff adder Hiding in long grasses at night, this snake attacks rodents with its long fangs and highly poisonous venom.

DAYTIME

During daylight hours, the richest grazing grounds on the continent come alive with some of Africa's most iconic beasts. When the sun has passed its highest point in the sky, many of these creatures stop their search for food and congregate around a single place: the waterhole. Here, giraffes, elephants, ostriches, and wildebeests gather to drink, often under the watchful eye of their predators. This is rush hour in the Serengeti, and there is safety in numbers for a brief moment when the need for water is more important than finding food.

READ about the species below and then turn back to THE OBSERVATION DECK.
Looking through the RED lens, what can you see?

Cheetah The fastest creature on the planet hunts its food in broad daylight, chasing and tripping its prey at high speed.

African elephant The plains' largest land mammal has complex communication systems, alerting family members to food and predators.

Ostrich This giant land bird has strong leg muscles and can maintain high speeds to escape the pursuit of hungry predators.

Giraffe With a tongue 18 inches long, the world's tallest mammal eats leaves from the acacia tree for most of its waking hours.

Banded mongoose This nomadic hunter finds shelter in termite mounds, and can be heard chattering throughout the day.

Blue wildebeest This great traveler of the plains is continually on the move, always seeking fresh grass and water.

African tree hyrax After a morning sunbath, this furry mammal feeds in circles, facing outward to spot danger.

Klipspringer This "rock jumper" mates for life, feeding and drinking on the succulents and plants of the Serengeti plains.

Olive baboon Africa's most common primate can be spotted here in groups of up to 40, feeding on plants and small insects.

THE GANGES RIVER BASIN

Sacred to Hindus around the world, the Ganges River is home to hundreds of animal species – and over 400 million people. Rising in the Himalayas and emptying into the Bay of Bengal, it drains one-fourth of the territory of India, and its surrounding fertile soils are prime growth areas for rice, sugar cane, oilseeds, lentils, wheat, and potatoes. The creatures that live in its waters and neighboring forests and mangroves must contend with human activity around the river. Animals like the Ganges river dolphin have learned to live around many river and man-made dam systems, though not without cost to its species, with less than 1,800 now living in the wild.

WELCOME TO THE RIVER

Destination
The Ganges River Basin

Continent
Asia

Countries
India, Bangladesh

Habitat
River, Forests, Mangroves

Size
420,000 square miles

Who lives here
219 aquatic species, 315 bird species, 176 fish, and 31 crustacean species. There are also 35 reptile and 42 mammal species, and it is home to the world's last population of the Bengal tiger.

NIGHTTIME AND TWILIGHT

As the bright hum of human activity starts to fade, light turns to dark and the river's hunters wake up for the night. Lying low in its shallows, the fish-eating crocodile is perfectly poised to spot breakfast, with eyes, ears, and nostrils located on top of its head. This predator stays almost totally submerged and hidden as it searches for food, using its smell and night vision to capture reflections on the water's surface. Like all other creatures that call this river home, this crocodile must navigate areas of the river heavily polluted with human and industrial waste to find nourishing meals.

READ about the species below and then turn back to THE OBSERVATION DECK.
Looking through the BLUE lens, what can you see?

Ganges shark Like other sharks, this mysterious creature relies on hearing, smell, and electroreception to find food.

Wildcat Inhabiting the forest adjacent to the Ganges, this feline feeds on reptiles, insects, and amphibians of the river system.

Sloth bear This bear is a good swimmer and marks its forest territory by scratching tree trunks with its forepaws.

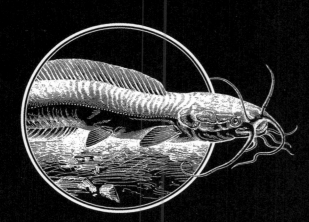

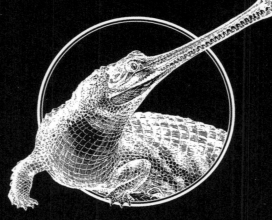

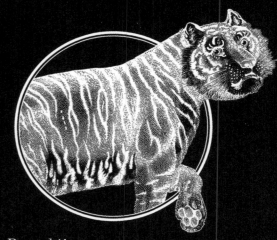

Walking catfish This freshwater fish uses its stiffened pectoral fins to wriggle upright to find food.

Fish-eating crocodile This species has an elongated, narrow snout that reduces resistance to water when hunting fish.

Bengal tiger The biggest member of the tiger family hides before ambushing wild mammals of the river's nearby forest.

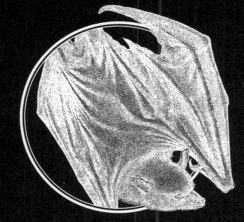

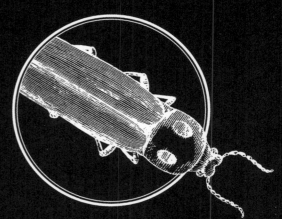

Flying fox Also known as a fruit bat, this species uses smell to locate blossoms, pollen, and fruit of the river's nearby trees.

Golden jackal Hunting in pairs, this canine runs along both sides of streams, driving prey from one jackal to the other.

Firefly This insect produces a chemical reaction that allows it to light up, attracting a mate and warding off predators.

DAYTIME

Even before the sun has risen fully, the river is awake and bustling with life. Every creature that navigates in daylight must adapt to the frenetic life of the river and human activity nearby. The Ganges river dolphin, a rare species of dolphin that is considered blind at birth, must surface every five minutes to breathe air. Fishing nets and low river flow have meant that numbers of this species have dwindled, putting it on the endangered list. Many efforts are being made to preserve this wild species, and sustain the rich variety of creatures that call the river home.

READ about the species below and then turn back to THE OBSERVATION DECK. Looking through the RED lens, what can you see?

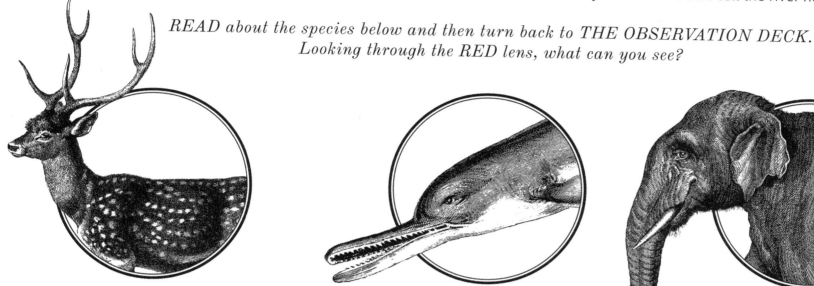

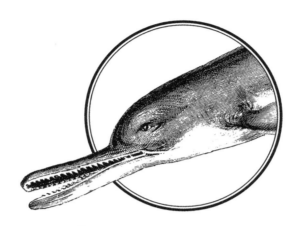

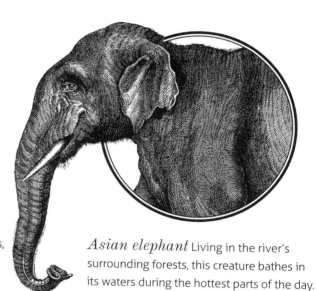

Chital deer Hunted by the Bengal tiger, this spotted deer can run at speeds of up to 40 miles per hour to escape.

Ganges river dolphin Active at all hours, this species can be spotted in daylight using calls and echoes to navigate the river.

Asian elephant Living in the river's surrounding forests, this creature bathes in its waters during the hottest parts of the day.

Lesser florican During the rainy season, or "monsoon", the male of this species performs a leaping ritual to woo females.

Indian softshell turtle This turtle has adapted to survive in the river – it's a strong swimmer and can breathe underwater.

Kingfisher Hovering over the river before diving for food, this small fishing bird feasts on the diverse life found in the Ganges.

Black-necked stork With a spear-sharp beak, this water bird stands in the shallows and hunts fish and insects.

Greater spotted eagle A guest to the river's wetlands in winter, this bird of prey hunts fish and small reptiles while in flight.

Mynah bird A member of the starling family, the male of this species performs an elaborate aerial routine to attract a female.

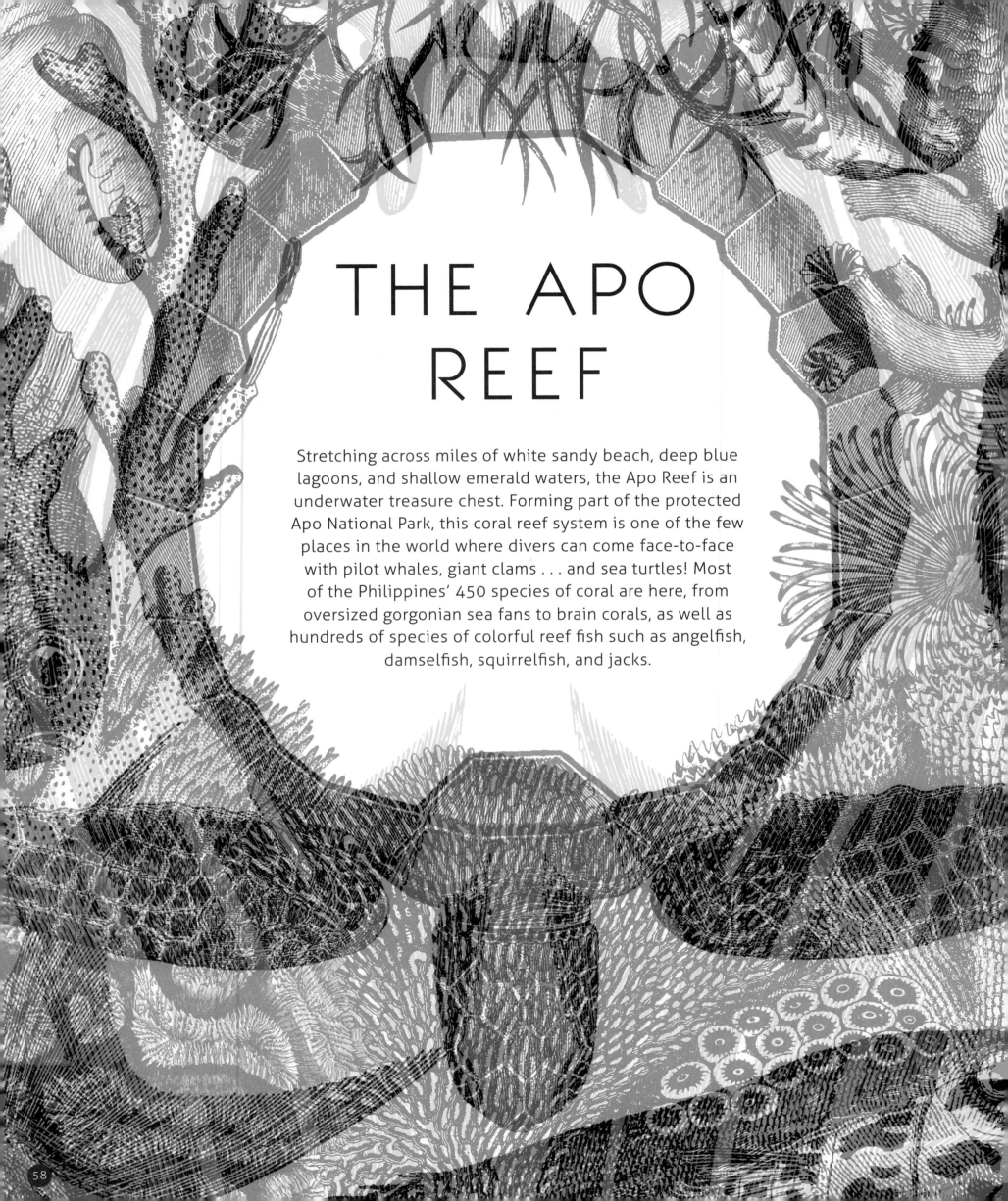

THE APO REEF

Stretching across miles of white sandy beach, deep blue lagoons, and shallow emerald waters, the Apo Reef is an underwater treasure chest. Forming part of the protected Apo National Park, this coral reef system is one of the few places in the world where divers can come face-to-face with pilot whales, giant clams . . . and sea turtles! Most of the Philippines' 450 species of coral are here, from oversized gorgonian sea fans to brain corals, as well as hundreds of species of colorful reef fish such as angelfish, damselfish, squirrelfish, and jacks.

WELCOME TO THE CORAL REEF

Destination
The Apo Reef

Continent
Asia

Country
The Philippines

Habitat
Coral Reef

Size
13 square miles

Who lives here
Green turtles, endangered hawksbill turtles, short-finned pilot whales, bottlenose dolphins, as well as 285 species of fish and 450 species of coral.

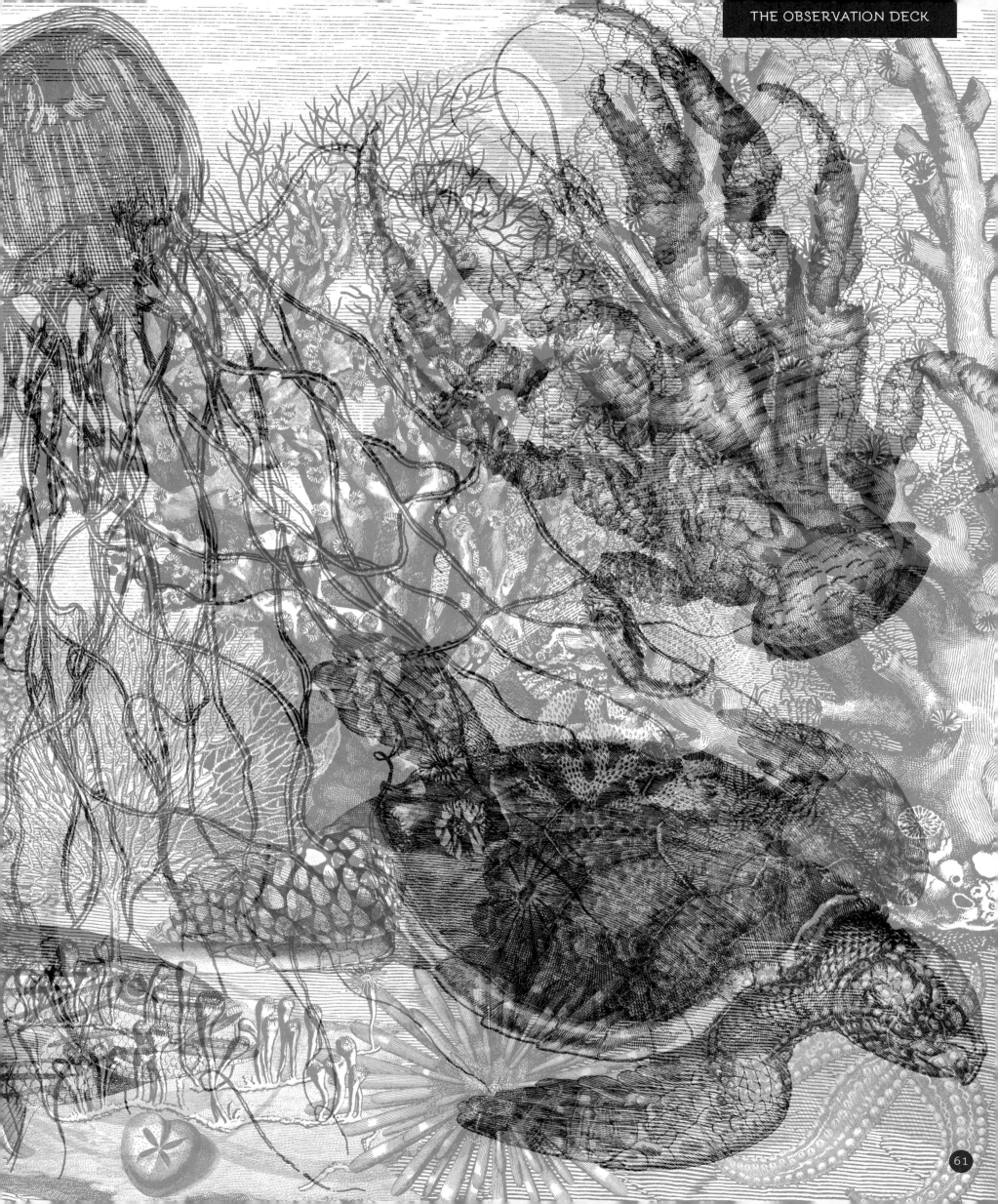

NIGHTTIME AND TWILIGHT

As dusk settles upon the blue sapphire seas of the reef, the nighttime creatures begin their day. Less colorful than their daytime cousins, the dark night provides cover for a host of reef creatures, allowing them to emerge from their daytime shelters with some chance of remaining undetected. Many of these creatures have large eyes, boosted by a reflective layer within the eye that allows them to gather as much of the faint light as possible. A lot of hatching is controlled by light levels, and many reef creatures make their entrance into the world in the hour following dusk.

READ about the species below and then turn back to THE OBSERVATION DECK.
Looking through the BLUE lens, what can you see?

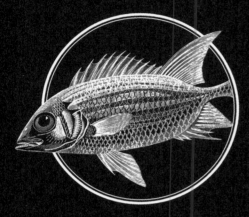

Squirrelfish During a night hunt, this species produces sounds with its swimbladder for communications.

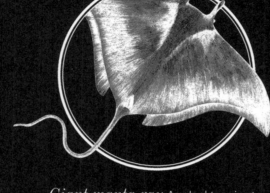

Giant manta ray As plankton rise to the water's surface at night, they are met by the manta ray, which feasts by moonlight.

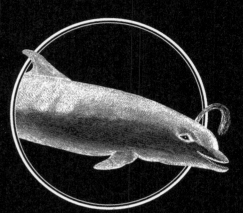

Bottlenose dolphin Active both day and night, twilight is the busiest and most vocal feeding time for this dolphin.

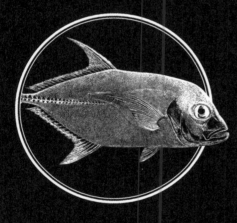

Black jack fish Hiding in crevices in the outer reef during the day, this creature feeds in groups of up to 30 at night.

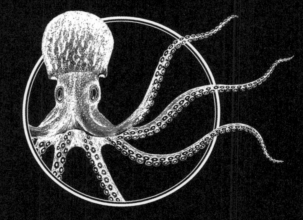

Ornate octopus Poking its tentacles down holes in coral, this hunter literally flushes out its food each night.

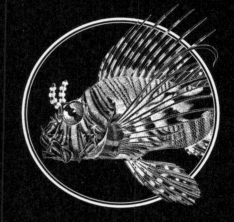

Spotfin lionfish The whispy spines that cover this fish are venomous, stinging predators that get too close.

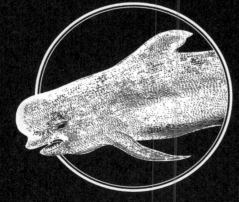

Short-finned pilot whale Known as the "cheetah of the deep", this whale pursues its breakfast of squid at high speeds.

Catfish This highly attuned species can determine the origin of reef sounds, and from which direction they came.

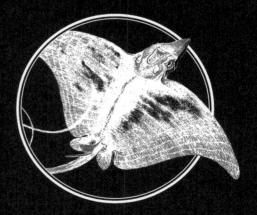

Eagle ray Cruising in the shallows, this ray's wings break the water's surface, giving the impression of sharks traveling together.

DAYTIME

By the time the sun has reached the three islands of the Apo Natural Park, it's rush hour in the reef's underwater city. Flooded with light, the reef is a feeding ground for daytime workers, whose brightly colored appearance carries information for territorial rivals, schoolmates, and breeding partners. The different types of workers hunt in different areas of the reef: grazers and invertebrates favor the sand bed of the reef, while plankton-feeders head into the current to reap the drifting prey particles.

READ about the species below and then turn back to THE OBSERVATION DECK.
Looking through the RED lens, what can you see?

Hawksbill sea turtle Though most active in daylight, babies of this species hatch at night and crawl into the sea.

Green sea turtle Named for the color of its skin, this turtle is known to take to land to sunbathe, sometimes alongside seals!

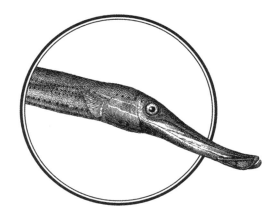

Trumpetfish To deceive prey, this fish camouflages itself as a floating stick by hanging vertically among seaweed.

Damselfish The male of this species performs a "signal jump" before its mate, rising and then swimming rapidly downward.

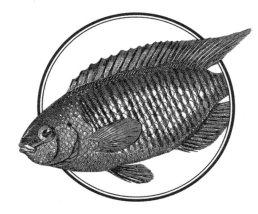

Green chromis Camouflaged by apple-green and light blue scales, this species is hunted by groupers and lionfish in daylight.

Bluestripe snapper This yellow creature is known to swim alongside goatfish during the day for extra protection from predators.

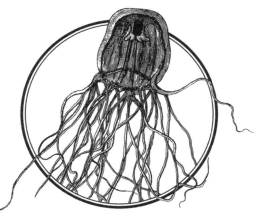

Box jellyfish Hunting in daylight, this creature is the most venomous marine creature known to man.

Giant clam By day, this clam opens its shell so that the algae it feeds on receive the daily shot of sunlight they need to grow.

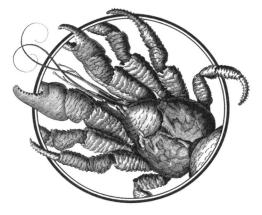

Coconut crab Active by day and night, this creature is called the "robber crab" because of its habit of climbing trees to steal coconuts.

First published in the U.S. in 2016 by
Wide Eyed Editions, an imprint of Quarto Inc.,
276 Fifth Avenue, Suite 206, New York, NY 10001
QuartoKnows.com
Visit our blogs at QuartoKnows.com

ISBN 978-1-84780-887-5

The artworks were drawn digitally using scanned pencil textures
Set in DIN Alternate, DIN bold, and Mrs Green

Designed by Nicola Price
Edited by Jenny Broom
Production by Laura Grandi
Published by Rachel Williams

Printed in Dongguan, Guangdon, China

1 3 5 7 9 8 6 4 2